The Clever Little Tailor and other stories

Adapted by Sheila Lane and Marion Kemp

Illustrations by Joy FitzSimmons

Take Part Starters

Level 1

Ward Lock Educational Co. Ltd.

Ward Lock Educational Co. Ltd.
1, Christopher Road
East Grinstead
Sussex
RH19 3BT

A member of the Ling Kee Group
London • New York • Hong Kong • Singapore

© Sheila Lane and Marion Kemp
This edition published 1991
ISBN 0 7062 5153 9

Printed in Hong Kong

Contents

★ This sign means
that you can make
the sounds which
go with the story.

The Clever Little Tailor

This is the little tailor who hit at a swarm of flies and killed seven at one blow.

This is the giant

The little tailor is walking along the road with a soft, round cheese in his pocket.

Tailor I want everyone to know
I killed SEVEN AT ONE BLOW.
I may be little, but I'm clever. . .
What's this? It's a bird in a trap.
All right, little bird. I'll put you in my
pocket.

Giant Got you!

Tailor You great, big bully. Let me go.

Giant No, no! I am going to keep you.

Tailor You won't want to keep me when you read what it says on my vest. Look! It says, SEVEN AT ONE BLOW.

Giant SEVEN. . .AT. . .ONE. . .BLOW.

Tailor I may be little, but I'm clever.
SEVEN AT ONE BLOW,
SO LET ME GO!

Giant No, no! I am going to keep you.

Tailor I think you're just a great big bully. Will you let me go if I show you that I am a very clever fellow?

Giant What can a little man like you do?

Tailor I can squeeze water out of a stone. Look! I happen to have a cheese stone in my pocket. Watch me squeeze the water out. Drip! Drip! ★

Giant How can a little man like you
do that?

Tailor I told you. I'm a very clever fellow.
So now will you let me go?

Giant No, no! I am going to keep you.

Tailor You really are a great big bully! Will
you let me go if I can throw a stone
farther than you can?

Giant A little man like you cannot do that.

Tailor Oh, yes I can. But you must throw
your stone first. Pick it up. I'll count
to three and then you must throw.
One. . .two. . .three. . .THROW!

Giant There! Look at that!

Tailor That wasn't bad. But now watch me!
You can do the counting this time.

Giant Yes! One. . .two. . .three. . .GO!

Tailor Look at that! It's going farther and farther into the sky. . . It's gone out of sight. . . and it still hasn't come back. Now will you let me go?

Giant No, no! I am going to keep you.

Tailor You must be the biggest bully in the world. What else can I do? I know! You see that big oak tree which has been blown down by the wind?

Giant Yes, I can see it.

Tailor Will you promise to let me go if I can carry the heavy end while you carry the light end?

Giant Yes, I will let you go if you can carry the heavy end.

Tailor Now you've promised! You take the trunk end on your back and I'll take the heavy leaves and branches.

Giant I have my end, but I cannot see you.

Tailor That's because you can't turn round. I'm here all right. Keep on walking. Remember, I've got the heavy end.

Giant My end is heavy too.

Tailor Don't say you can't carry it! Are you going to put it down already?

Giant Yes, I am.
It is too heavy.
It is going to fall.
Look out!

Tailor CRASH! ★
Now. . .
Did I squeeze water out of a stone!

Giant Yes, you did.

Tailor Did I throw a stone so high that it didn't come back?

Giant Yes, you did.

Tailor Did I carry the heavy end of a tree?

Giant Yes, you did.

Tailor So keep your promise and let me go, FOR I KILLED SEVEN AT ONE BLOW

And off ran the Clever Little Tailor who used his brains to get away from the Giant.

Things for you to do

1

This is the Clever Little
Tailor's vest.

What would you have
on your vest?
Draw your vest and
write your words on it.

2 A giant is *big.* An oak tree is *big.*
Write: *big* on your paper.
Draw things which are big.

The Little Tailor is *little.* A fly is *little.*
Write: *little* on your paper.
Draw things which are little.

3 Write these sentences in the right order for the story.

Next the Little Tailor let the bird fly in the sky.
Last he made the Giant carry the big end of the tree.
First the Little Tailor squeezed the cheese.

4 How many things can you think of that fly in the sky?

Draw the pictures and write the names.

The Town Mouse and the Country Mouse

This is the Town Mouse.

This is his friend,
the Country Mouse.

The Town Mouse has come to visit the Country Mouse who lives in a nest of grass at the side of a field.

Town Mouse So this is where my country friend lives. What a poor little place! I'll call out to him. ANYONE AT HOME?

Country Mouse Yes, yes. I am at home.

Town Mouse So this is where you hide yourself away. Can I come in?

Country Mouse Yes, yes. Come in.

Town Mouse Dear me! What a poor little place you live in. There isn't room to swing a cat in here!

Country Mouse Cat! Cat! Don't say that!

Town Mouse I'm sorry. I didn't mean to frighten you.

Country Mouse Don't say cat! You must not say that!

Town Mouse Dear me! You are a frightened little thing. I don't suppose you have many visitors down here.

Country Mouse No, I don't, but it is good to see you.

Town Mouse Well, now that I'm here let's have a good time. I feel like having a little cheese and wine.

Country Mouse Cheese and wine! But I have no cheese and wine.

Town Mouse Dear me! No cheese and wine! I suppose you've lived on corn since the day you were born. Come along! Let's go to my place in the town and I'll give you a fine time.

Country Mouse That is very good of you, but . . .

Town Mouse Don't worry! Care killed the cat! Oh dear! I mustn't say that! Let's go.

Town Mouse Come along in and make yourself at home, my dear friend.

Country Mouse So this is where you live.

Town Mouse Isn't it grand?

Country Mouse I have never seen a house like this.

Town Mouse Jellies, cakes, cheese!
Eat as much as you please.

Country Mouse It looks very good but . . .

Town Mouse I knew you would enjoy life in the town.

Country Mouse Oh! Oh! What was that? ★ Was it a cat?

Town Mouse Follow me and we'll see.

Country Mouse I don't like this at all.

Town Mouse It's only the cook. She will be gone in a moment. Don't be frightened.

Country Mouse I would like to go home.
I'm a country mouse.
I don't like this house.

Town Mouse She's gone! She's gone!
Now, back to the feast.
Jellies, cakes, cheese!
Eat as much as you please.

Country Mouse It looks very good, but . . .

Town Mouse I knew you would enjoy life in the town.

Country Mouse Oh! Oh! What was that? ★
Was it a cat?

Town Mouse Follow me and we'll see.

Country Mouse I don't like this at all.

Town Mouse   It's only the dog. He will be gone
in a moment.
Don't be frightened.

Country Mouse   I would like to go home.
I'm a country mouse.
I don't like this house.

Town Mouse   He's gone! He's gone!
Now, back to the feast.
Jellies, cakes, cheese!
Eat as much as you please.

Country Mouse It looks very good, but. . .

Town Mouse I knew you would enjoy life in the town.

Country Mouse Oh! Oh! What was that? ★ Was it a cat?

Town Mouse Follow me and we'll see.

Country Mouse I don't like this at all.

23

Town Mouse It's only the cat!

Country Mouse CAT! CAT!
I'm not staying here.
I'm a country mouse
And I like my own house.
I'm off!
Goodbye!

*Would you rather be a Country Mouse
or a Town Mouse?*

Things for you to do

1

Draw five kinds of homes.

This is the home of the Country Mouse.

a house

2 A country mouse can make its nest just above the ground.
Write: *Things which live above the ground* on your paper.
Draw things which live above the ground.

3 Write the sentences in the right order for the story.

Last the two mice heard the sound of a cat.
First the two mice heard the sound of the cook.
Next the two mice heard the sound of the dog.

4 How many things can you think of which you can eat?

Draw the pictures and write the names.

The Boy who flew too near the Sun

This is the boy.   This is the boy's father.

A father and his son are standing between some high rocks on an island.

Father The king of this island is a bad man. He has left us here between these high rocks because he thinks that we cannot climb out.

Son I can climb out.

Father No, my son. When you climb these rocks, you will just see more rocks.

Son So I will climb more rocks.

Father On the other side of the great rocks is the great sea. We have no ship and it is too far to swim to our home in Greece.

Son We will go home one day, father.

Father No, my son. I think we shall have to stay here for ever.

Son I will not stay here for ever.

Father What will you do then? You have no wings, so you cannot fly like a bird.

Son No, I cannot fly like a bird.

Father Even the bees can fly up to their nests in the rocks.
Even the bees are free.

Son The birds have wings.
The bees have wings.
I wish. . .I wish. . .I wish I had wings.

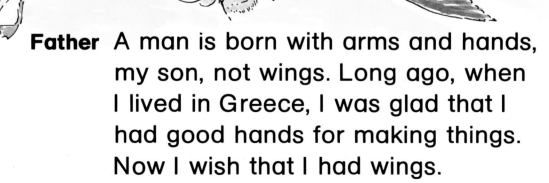

Father A man is born with arms and hands, my son, not wings. Long ago, when I lived in Greece, I was glad that I had good hands for making things. Now I wish that I had wings.

28

Son You can still make things, father.

Father What can I make here?
I have no tools.

Son You *can* make something, father.
You can make something for me.

Father What can I make for you, my son?

Son You can make me some wings.

Father Wings! Wings! Are you mad?
I cannot make anything without
tools, so how can I make wings?

Son You have hands, father.
Your hands can be your tools.

Father What can I use for feathers?

Son Look! Here is a feather. . .
Look! Here is another one. . .

Father Yes, there are many seabirds'
feathers on the rocks, but tell me
this – how can feathers be stuck
together to make wings?

Son Look up there!

Father What are you looking at? I can only
see a swarm of bees flying in and
out of their nest in the rocks.

Son And in the nest there is. . .

Father WAX! Of course! The wax of a bee is a kind of glue. When bees' wax is warmed, it is soft and sticky. But when wax cools it sets and becomes hard.

Son So you *can* make wings, father.

Father I have hands for tools, birds' feathers for wings and bees' wax for glue. My son! We will try to make some wings.

Son I will climb up and get the wax.

Father And I will collect feathers. There are so many on the rocks, but I had never thought of using them to make wings. My son is a clever boy. Perhaps, one day. . .

Son Father! Father!

Father What is it, my son?

Son Look! I have the wax.

Father And it is still soft and sticky. Let us put it on this flat rock. Now, go and get some more feathers and I will begin to make the wings.

Son I will go.

Father Hurry, my son. The wax is beginning to get hard.

Son Here is some more wax and here are some more feathers.

Father Put the wax on the flat rocks and lay the feathers on like this. . .When the wax is hard, we will climb on to that high rock and see if we can fly.

Son I have seen the birds fly, father, so I can fly too.

Father Listen, my son. You must not try to fly too soon.

Son Let me try my wings soon, father. Let me try them soon.

Father Listen to me, boy. You must be careful. At first you must not try to fly too far. Then you must not fly too near the sun. Remember that.

Son I will, I will, but let me try my wings.

Father The wax is hard now. Stand still and I will tie the wings on your arms with the cord we wear for belts.

Son And I will tie wings on your arms too, father.

Father Do not be in such a hurry. We must be careful in everything we do, if we are to be free.

Son I want to be free.
　　　Now that I have wings I *can* be free.

Father We will climb up to that high rock
　　　above us. Now, take care, my son!

Son I will. . .I will. . .
　　　Look! There is the sea.

Father Listen to the waves crashing on to the rocks. ★ You must fly high above the waves, my son.

Son I will. I will.

Father But do not go so high that you fly near the great sun.

Son Father! Father!
Look at me!
I can fly!

Father Take care, my son! Take care!
Yes. . .he flies like a bird.
My son can fly!

Son I can fly!
I can fly!
Father! Father!
Come too!

Father I'm coming, my son. I'm coming. . .

Son Look at me!
I can fly up into the sky.
I will fly up to the sun.

Father No! NO! Come back! Come back!
You must not fly too near the sun!
COME BACK!

Son Up, up and away I go.

Father Come back! COME BACK!. . .
The feathers are falling out. . .
The heat from the sun is melting
the wax. . .
My son! My son! COME BACK!. . .
Too late! He is falling like a stone.
Down! Down! Down! ★
He has fallen beneath the waves.
My son has gone.
There is only one feather left
floating on the waves.
My son is lost to me for ever.

The boy, whose name was Icarus, drowned in the sea. His father flew sadly home to Greece alone.

Things for you to do

1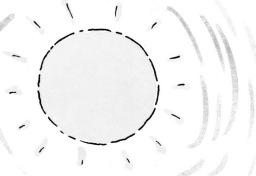

Draw five things which give us light.

The boy flew too near the sun.
The sun gives us light.

a candle

2 The sun is *hot.*
Write: *hot* on your paper.
Draw things which are hot.

Ice is *cold.*
Write: *cold* on your paper.
Draw things which are cold.

3 Write these sentences in the right order for the story.

Next he got the wax.
Then he put the wax on a flat rock.
First the boy climbed up to the bees' nest.

4 How many things can you think of that *sink* in water?

Draw the pictures and write the names.